FROM PRISON TO PERIWINKLES

HOPE BEYOND ADDICTION

JASON HEAD

STREAMLINE
BOOKS

I would like to dedicate this book to my mom, the woman who never gave up on me. Thank you for everything you have done in my life and for believing in me when I did not believe in myself. I love you.

CONTENTS

Foreword   vii
by Cristi Hlavaty

My Heart Behind Writing   ix

1. Do You Need This Book?   1
2. The Beginning of My First Life   11
3. The World You Don't See   21
4. Bottomed Out   37
5. Life Behind Bars   51
6. Enough. Enough. Enough.   59
7. Hurry Up and Wait   71
8. Life Begins at Forty-four   81
9. Why Me?   97
10. My Hope for Me and My Hope for You   105

Acknowledgments   117
About the Author   119

FOREWORD
BY CRISTI HLAVATY

I first met Jason in the mid-80s while attending the same high school in Mesquite, Texas. I did not know him very well back then, but I remember he had the most piercing blue eyes I had ever seen. It would not be until 2019 that I would get to know him and learn the real truth behind drug addiction. His story is so inspiring and has awakened compassion in me to learn about and understand the devastating effects of drug abuse that are so often misunderstood. I have had the honor of attending meetings, recovery programs, and speaking engagements with Jason, where he courageously dives into real-life events, the vicious cycle of crime, and the degrading and humiliating lifestyle he lived in pursuit of a daily high.

With the turn of every page, Jason tells the story of how he survived the dark world of drug addiction, escaped death multiple times, endured life behind bars, and broke free with the help of his mom's unconditional love and support. His compelling comeback story will leave you feeling like anything is possible. Every day is a new chance to start your life over, and it's never too late. I pray that this book finds its way to you and gives you hope beyond anything measurable. Whether you are the one needing help, or you have a family member or friend in harm's way, this book will give you insight into the life of an addict. You will see that overcoming the difficult obstacles blocking the road to sobriety and maintaining a life without drugs is possible. This inspiring story will give any reader hope that anything can be achieved if you want it badly enough and are willing to put in the work. You are worth it. You can do it. No amount of shame or guilt will ever be greater than God's grace.

MY HEART BEHIND WRITING

There is a lot of stuff that I've done in this life that I wish I could wish away. But I can't. Moving forward is hard when it feels like you can never escape your past.

But that's my *why* behind writing this book: to show people that you can move forward despite your failures. It's not easy and it's not always fun. But once you change your mindset and–more than that–change the posture of your heart, that's when your trajectory can flip itself right side up.

I tried to be the realest version of myself in the pages ahead. You will read about my greatest failures, worst decisions, and most difficult moments. You will see my heart and mind transform right before your eyes (with a little help from my long-lost friend: Sobriety). And gradually, you will see that there is hope to be found in every situation. No two stories are the same, but I believe that I dug myself into a larger hole than the average Joe; so I hope that you can see that if I can do it, then you can too.

In the second-half of the book, you will notice four sections titled "Never Too Late". These points in the book are places where I wanted to take a moment to reflect on a certain aspect of my story. The four key areas of emphasis and empowerment in my testimony are:

- Recovering from Addiction
- Post-Prison Life
- Follow Your Dream
- Forgiveness from Yourself and Others

There is redemption for all of us—should we choose it. It's never too late.

FROM PRISON TO
PERIWINKLES

1

DO YOU NEED THIS BOOK?

THERE ARE BAD DAYS, THERE ARE WORSE DAYS, AND THEN THERE'S this particular day in May of 2011. I was lying on my mom's couch in Mesquite, Texas, feeling totally out of it. That part alone wasn't unusual. I was thirty-six years old, and at that point I'd been a hard core drug addict for over twenty years. Feeling strung out was pretty much my normal operating state. But this time I wasn't just high. Two weeks before I had been gunned down and nearly died. As I laid there, I still felt half dead. Pus was oozing out of my eight bandaged wounds. See, I got shot four times, but each bullet went in *and* out so that's eight holes in my body and they hurt like hell. The hospital prescribed opioids for the pain and now I'm addicted to those, so my prescription isn't nearly enough. Luckily, even stuck here alone at my mom's house I can still score them; it pays to know everyone in the drug game. The same drug game that led to two different guys firing on me, one with a nine millimeter and the other with a forty caliber. Two bullets ripped through my lung, collapsing it, and the other two wreaked havoc on my left arm. Technically, I got shot five times, but the fifth was just birdshot pellets from a twelve-gauge shotgun and that injury was nothing compared to the others. The last fourteen days have been the worst pain of my life. I've been through plenty of dustups and drag-outs in my life, but nothing comes close to recovering from this. There's literally a hole in my sternum. The pain is hard-core.

When I was in the hospital, it took me a week and a half until I could even take a couple steps again. And then they kicked me out a couple days after that! I definitely do not feel like I should be at home and on my own right now. But when I was in the hospital they looked at me like I was a piece of crap. I get it, they saw a strung out drug addict who had no respect for life. If they looked at my medical records, they'd see this wasn't even close to the first time I had almost got myself killed. In fact, this time I died twice in the ambulance on the way to the hospital. They probably decided I wasn't really worth their effort. And of course, I didn't have health insurance, so I'm sure they figured they'd never see a dime for the medical bills I was racking up and wanted to cut that off as soon as possible.

So they discharged me, and I'm back at my mom's house whether I feel like I'm ready or not. Physically, I'm at my lowest. I'm so weak—six-foot-three and only about 170 pounds due to both my injuries and my destructive lifestyle in general. Mentally, it's not any better. I'm in a dark place, so depressed and so lonely. I know my family and friends feel sympathy for me, but I also know they don't feel safe being around me, and I get it. They don't want to get caught in the crossfire. I mean, several different people literally just tried to kill me. And you'd better believe I feel like a sitting duck lying here helpless, waiting for them to come and finish the job. When the ambulance brought me to the hospital, they checked me in under the name "XYZ Jason Head". That's how they do it when someone gets shot and the shooter is still on the loose. So some homicidal maniac can't come into the facility and easily find you. Even my Facebook got shut down to try to keep me safe and my location a secret. Since I don't know who it was that tried to kill me, I'm completely paranoid, and I've changed locations between the houses of family members a couple times already. Since I've gotten to my mom's, I've been showering while squatted down in a crouched position. Like literally shampooing my hair on my knees to stay out of view of the high little window in the shower. I've been begging my mom not to walk in front of the windows too. The fact that she still stays with me in that house proves beyond any doubt that she is actually a saint.

Prison visitation with mom in 2008.

But my mom is at work, and I am on that couch, bandaged up and lying there in misery. My thoughts are swimming, feeling full of guilt and shame for not being the person I should be. My own private pity party in my own self-made hell, and then I hear something ... someone's knocking at the front door. Shit. I force myself off the couch and crawl to a window and peek out. I can see a white Ford F250 truck parked outside, and I make out the outline of a gardener's hat. I breathe a sigh of relief. This guy must be working and clearly just has the wrong house. I pull open the front door, and the cold barrel of a gun goes straight to my forehead. Nope, not the wrong house. This is definitely meant for me. I knew they would find me.

I know people always say their lives flash before their eyes, but at the moment this was happening I was so out of it that it didn't even feel real. I think I was still in some heavy post-traumatic stress from being shot. And, of course, I was strung out. So even though I'm standing there with a gun to my head, everything just feels kind of blurry. He pulls the trigger ... click.

Nothing happens. The gun is jammed. I take the opportunity and grab the barrel, and we tussle to the ground. Normally I'd have him, but I'm weak as hell right now. He probably did a bump right before he came in, so he's whacked out and not in the greatest shape either. I've always been a fighter and can usually handle myself, but at 170 pounds soaking wet, I'm not in any condition to be wrestling with a meth'ed out maniac. He gets the gun back and gets to his feet and points the barrel at me again. Click click. Still jammed.

As I lay there considering my options (nope, there really aren't any), I hear the dude making a call. He's talking to someone, explaining what happened with the gun, and asking what he should do about it. Of course at the time I assumed this was related to the guys that tried to kill me two weeks before, but I would find out later that I'd been framed for something else and this guy was trying to kill me for something I actually *didn't* even do! Karmically, though, I have it coming for what I *have* done. Part of me just wants him to finish the job and get it over with. This life isn't even worth living anymore. I lie there and wait for my inevitable fate.

It doesn't come. Apparently, whoever he was on the phone with tells him to leave, 'cause he suddenly gets in the truck and takes off. I guess I'm not gonna meet my maker today. I guess someone or something has another plan for me. Surely, this time I'm gonna turn my life around. It can't get more rock bottom than this, can it? Ha. Nope. It takes four more years of this until I finally make that change.

If you had told me twenty years ago I would be writing a book to inspire others to turn their lives around, I'd have laughed in your face. Then I might have punched you in the face, taken your money, and used it to buy more drugs. Nah, just kidding about that one. I never robbed any old ladies, mostly just people in the drug world that were doing dirty or doing something illegal. Not that it makes it any better, because it doesn't, but I guess I had some kind of moral values. And also, someone in the drug world isn't going to go to the police, they're just going to take revenge. You know when you watch an action movie and there's the thug who kicks down the door of a dope house? The tatted-up guy with ripped muscles and guns blazing? Yep. That was me. For decades. Not anymore, though. I'm an ex-thug-hugs-not-drugs kind of guy now. Who'd have thunk it.

I'll tell you who. My mom. She was the only one who

never gave up on me. So for the purpose of this book consider me your "mom". Your six-foot-three, 255-pound, tattooed mom with a prison record a mile long. I haven't given up on you either. I'm telling you that no matter what you've done, no matter what ditch you are lying in right now, no matter how deep the shit is that you are stuck in, it's not too late. I'm forty-eight years old. And my life didn't really start until I was forty-four. That's right, I wasted decades of my life. Today I'm like a middle-aged sixteen year old finally growing up and being the person I was always supposed to be. And my life is frickin' fantastic now. So here's the good news: It's never too late to hit the reset button if you want to. I know, your reset button might be hidden down deep, all rusty and grown over with weeds and dirt. Well, get a shovel and dig it out. I promise you, it will still work. But only you can press the button; I can't do it for you. Even a six-foot-three tatted-up substitute-mom-of-a-man can't make you change. But I'll tell you this—if I can do it you sure as hell can too. I spent a total of fifteen years and eight months in different prisons for a variety of crimes. I almost died numerous times. My name meant nothing but trouble to people and I disappointed everyone that ever knew me and loved me. So if I can turn it around, you can too.

In the last four years I have started a business, Headz Up Landscaping, and grown it from one lawnmower to one of the most respected landscaping businesses in the area. Last year I did over a million dollars in sales. And I literally just started a new business, Headz Up Roofing and Construction. I make great money, and to be straight, this is the first "real" job I've ever had. I have a house, a small fleet of cars including the Lamborghini of my dreams, and I'm able to take care of my family and loved ones. I'm proud of what I've accomplished and the nice things I have, but what I'm most proud of is myself. It feels amazing to have a good reputation, to have my name mean something positive for the first time ever. I'm engaged to the woman of my dreams, actually, let's say beyond my wildest dreams. And my mom finally has a son she can be proud of. And all this is possible because I've been sober since December 25, 2015.

I'm gonna say it again, it's never too late. Do you want it?

2

THE BEGINNING OF MY
FIRST LIFE

I was born June 10, 1974, in Dallas, Texas. I rolled into this world at almost twelve pounds like a sumo baby bowling ball, ready to take out anything in my path. My poor mom, she's a tiny lady. I swear, I don't know how she carried a twelve pound turkey like me. I was the youngest of three kids and have an older brother and sister. To hear my mom tell it, I was full throttle from day one. Like a water hose turned on full blast, and that's how I still am today according to my fiancé. My poor mom. She had her hands full with me. She called me a bull in a china closet. I don't really remember early childhood but as I got into kindergarten I started playing soccer, football, baseball, and I was really good at all sports. My mom said I didn't have an off switch, but was boom-boom-boom all over the place. I just kept going nonstop all day until I crashed.

I was wild and rambunctious and it seemed like I was

always in the emergency room for something. If my brother dared me to jump off a roof, I was one hundred percent gonna do it— and end up with stitches. Or the time I busted my head open riding a wheelie on my sister's Huffy bicycle which ended in ... more stitches. Even a simple family dinner could wind up bloody, like the time when I was six and I fell back in my dining room chair sending my fork straight into the bottom of my chin. And that fork stayed stuck in there all the way to the hospital. You know those little punch cards you get at a frozen yogurt shop? Where if you buy nine yogurts the tenth one is free? Someone shoulda given my mom one of those for the E.R. when I was a kid. Nine sets of stitches paid for, and don't worry Mrs. Head, we'll sew up Jason this time for free.

I'm a mama's boy, straight up, and I wear that badge proudly. That woman has always bent over backwards for me, my brother, and my sister. But if you let them tell it, I was her favorite, 'cause I was the baby. She shows her love through food and is an awesome cook. She takes a lot of pride in her food, and you can taste it for sure. Even if she's making something that seems simple, like spaghetti, hers is gonna be off the charts. My mom worked as a secretary for a trucking company for a while, but for most of my childhood she was a stay-at-home mom. She is a woman who loves fiercely, man. Even when she was poor and down and out, she would find a way to buy me shoes or polo shirts or whatever I needed. Even if she had to borrow the money from my grandma or whatever, she always made sure that she went above and beyond.

My dad was in the Marine Corps, and you know the type. Practice hard! Be number one! All of that. You'd better believe we made our beds every day. Literally, to this day you could roll up on his garage uninvited and everything would be immaculate and in perfect order. I definitely see that I got that from him. In my closet today I make sure everything is always hanging the same direction in order of color and category. He instilled a lot of those Marine values in me. I've never met anyone who works as hard as my dad. For a long time he was a plumber, then later on he worked for General Motors. I remember him working seven days a week on that job. He would expect us to work hard too. Like when we were playing sports, he expected us to be number one. And man, he would bust our butts when he needed to.

My dad started me mowing the lawn when I was five years old. I guess it was destiny that I now have a land-scaping business, because from the time I was little I was always totally OCD about it. I would use the lawnmower to mow perfect stripes in the grass of the front yard. By the time I was ten, the yard would be so immaculate if a kid rode his bike through my lawn we were gonna fight. Fists were gonna fly, one hundred percent. It was a little over the top, for sure, but also I think this quality definitely serves me in my business today! I take great pride in my work.

My brother, Chris, is only eighteen months older than me and for a lot of our childhoods he was my partner in crime. Luckily for him, he never went on to live a life of crime like I did. He's got a successful plumbing business; he's a great guy. When we were kids, he gave me the nickname "Buck" because I had a buck tooth. Later on, everyone in my circles assumed that my nickname was Buck because I was "buck wild". I totally was, but that's not where the name came from. My sister, Monica, is four years older than me. She works in real estate and also does really well. I had a good time with both of them when I was a kid. Overall, "Buck" had a happy childhood. It's not like parenting today. We were Gen X kids. We'd take off on our bikes in the morning and our parents had no idea where we were going. They'd say, "Just be home before dark." You just stayed out of sight and could enjoy your freedom. But if you got caught doing something you weren't supposed to be doing, I still remember those spankings, you know what I mean?

A recent picture of my dad and brother.

When I was thirteen my parents got divorced, and things really changed. I think my brother and I were already at really tough ages, and when they split up we just went wild. My dad had always been the hard-core one. We were hard to tame, but he wasn't afraid to give us some whoopings. But he went to live on the other side of Dallas, and when he was not in the picture as much we ran the streets. My mom did the best she could, but she had a lot on her plate at that time. She was so stressed with the pressures of being a single parent, and she was having a really hard time financially. It was a perfect storm for teenage trouble.

I smoked my first joint at thirteen years old with my brother. Nothing earth-shattering there, a lot of kids do. And like it does for most people, it started out social. We had a group of about forty of us kids from the neighborhood. We would get together and party, drink, and smoke joints. I was instantly hooked. Of course, I didn't realize that right away. For a long time, I was a scrawny little stoner who told myself that it was "just marijuana" and I didn't "need" it, but I was already in denial. I think if you had ten different people with ten different genetics and they all smoked weed for the first time they would all react differently. I know a lot of people that can control their life and smoke pot now and then, in fact some of the guys I smoked with back then still smoke today and run hugely successful businesses, but that wasn't in the cards for me.

A lot of people might be able to handle it, but unfortunately some people turn into straight drug addicts like I
did. Just like when I was busting my head open poppin'
wheelies on my sister's bike, I went full throttle. And
maybe you could say I was somewhat of a functioning
addict for a while, but not for long.

If this book is somehow reaching you in your teens,
know this. When you start doing drugs that young, you're
damaging a brain that isn't fully developed yet. Those
drugs are gonna change and hinder the way your mind is
supposed to grow. Looking back, I never really gave myself
a chance at life, period. I would get high for anything. We
used to steal A/C refrigerant and do it right into our
mouths. We called it "wah-wah" 'cause that's all you'd
hear, and then you'd fall over on the ground. It was
extreme; I'm lucky I have any brain cells left. Maybe I
could have been a genius, but I'll never know. I'm lucky I
can tie my shoes today. By the time I was fourteen I was
snorting lines of coke, and by fifteen I was smoking full-
fledged crack. And that's crazy for someone that young. I
was a young kid, running around the worst parts of South
Dallas, in neighborhoods we had no business being in. I
remember stealing my mom's VCR and TV to buy drugs.
Hopefully, you guys know what a VCR is. Ask your parents.
How messed up is that? My poor mom, working and
struggling to take care of us and make ends meet and I'm
up in there stealing her shit. Back then I didn't feel bad
about it, but I sure do now. I don't know how many Louis

Vuitton purses I'll need to buy her today to make it up to her, but I'm gonna find out.

When you catch a dope charge it's called "delivery of a controlled substance" or "possession of a controlled substance" or whatever the crime is with the words "controlled substance". It makes a lot of sense to me because every charge I ever caught, every crime I ever committed, including assault, theft, robbery—all of them—I did while under the influence of a controlling substance. Cocaine and other hard stuff like heroin and meth, they completely controlled my life. A lot of the felonies I caught when I was under the influence of a bunch of Xanax. If you abuse prescription drugs like that, they are just as dangerous.

The very first time I ever got arrested was for stealing car parts off of a Union Pacific Railroad train. The railroad tracks were right out behind my mom's house. We were poor, my mom was poor, we were just a bunch of young dumb kids doing whatever it took to get money for drugs and alcohol. Since I was a first-time offender it wasn't that big of a deal, I just had to do some community service. So what did I do next time? I went full throttle. I stole thirteen ATVs, you know, those three wheeler motorbikes. Full throttle with half a brain. I was a freshman, standing in the middle of the cafeteria at West Mesquite High School, when two cops walked in. These officers were big guys, intimidating, and they threw the cuffs on me, boom, right there and then. They walked me out in front of everybody and took me straight to juvenile detention. I spent two weeks in the Dallas juvenile detention center and I'll never forget my first day. As my cell door slammed shut I heard the song "It Never Rains in Southern California" playing over the little speakers at the center. I still remember it so vividly, like a scene in a movie, the words of the song hitting me as the door was slamming shut, almost like life was happening in slow motion ... clang. It was a whole other world I was entering as a fourteen-year-old kid. And it just escalated and escalated from there.

When I was fifteen years old, I got put on "serious offenders" probation. Every Monday, Wednesday, and Friday I had to take a drug test. Not that I cared. I had the balls to walk into the probation department, again not just any probation department, the serious one, completely stoned with a joint still behind my ear. The probation officer, I'll never forget him, his name was Mr. Burrows, coincidentally was the same guy who arrested me at school. He says, "Mr. Head, can you turn around?" He grabs the joint out of my ear and slaps handcuffs on me again. And that's when he took me to a place called Dallas County Youth Village, and I stayed at the adolescent treatment unit there for six months.

Life at Dallas County Youth Village was like being in a real strict military-like boot camp. Everything was about structure. You're locked up with a bunch of rowdy hooligans, myself included, so it needed to be. A lot of these kids were raised without dads. Most came from rough urban areas. A lot of them, like me, were there because of drugs. Once I was in there, I finally hit my growth spurt and went from a scrawny kid to six-foot-three. That led to me being on the basketball team there and at fifteen years old, and I'm not saying I was some phenomenon, because I wasn't, but I could dunk. My mom would come to the games to support me and would buy all us little juvenile delinquents soda and stuff.

After I got out of Dallas County Youth Village, I went to live with my dad for a while. He did his best to help me out. I got my driver's license and started going to a new school. I did okay for a bit, but then started going to parties and getting into fights. I guess that was my reputation out there. I was known for fighting. And that's where I met a girl who I got pregnant at sixteen, which resulted in the birth of my daughter. I ended up getting another girl pregnant a few years later—this time I had a son. I'll talk more about them later on, but suffice it to say for now that I was not any type of dad to these kids. I couldn't be a dad while I was busy being a selfish, drug-addicted idiot who only cared about getting high. Not that the moms ended up wanting anything to do with me either. I was robbing and getting high and living that dangerous lifestyle.

In my teen years, I went to juvenile detention three times, I went to Dallas County Youth Village once, and I went to Timberland Psychiatric Hospital for twenty-eight days. I wish I had gotten "scared straight" or been ready to change, but my downward slide was just beginning.

3
THE WORLD YOU DON'T SEE

THE CRIME WORLD IS A WHOLE OTHER WORLD THAT EXISTS alongside the regular world. Most of the time, in my opinion like ninety-nine percent of the time, the crimes are drug-related. And if you've never been in that game, you probably don't notice that world in your day-to-day life. You mainly only see it on the news when they report people robbing or stealing or jacking. The prisons and jails and institutions are full of drug addicts, and unfortunately it's set up to be a never-ending cycle. Someone gets a drug charge, they get locked up. That person eventually gets out, but they never get rehabilitated, so inevitably they start getting high again, lose control again, and go back to prison again. They lose control because they are under the influence of a controlling substance. Are you starting to see the theme here?

Once I started down this destructive path, it was an

inevitable downward spiral that was gonna end one of two ways. I was on a crash course highway with only two exits: death or prison. The fact that I am still here to even tell this story is a miracle in itself. These drugs—crack, heroin, and meth—are "want me" drugs because they create this intense physical need that is so strong it will take power over everything. There is nothing you won't do to get them. Especially crack. When I was smoking crack, I would spend up to $10,000 a week. There isn't another "want me" drug out there that you're gonna spend more money on. It's expensive and the "want me" is so strong that you'll find ways to get that money. You will do the most desperate crimes to get it. Theft, robbery, prostitution, whatever it takes, because nothing else matters.

And just because it makes you desperate doesn't mean it makes you smart. I walked into a Lowe's hardware store one time, grabbed a chainsaw right off the shelf, took it straight up to the customer service desk and said, "Ma'am, I need to return this." And the manager had been watching me the whole time, because I'm sure I looked like a strung-out idiot. He busted me right then and there. Well I got all mad and insulted and said, "This will be the last time I ever shop here!" and walked out, which I can laugh about now. I was an idiot. But also, that wasn't me. The fact that I even thought at the time that it would work, that was the dope.

When you're addicted to dope, nothing else matters. We would walk right into the middle of a construction site looking for concrete saws. This would be in the middle of the day with people everywhere. Those saws are expensive, they cost around $1,500 apiece, and we could hawk them for 400 bucks. We'd go right into the middle of a job site, grab a saw in front of all these construction workers and take off running. Just desperate, desperate stuff and it just kept escalating and escalating.

I used to scope the parking lots of Home Depots looking for my next score. We'd steal those Toro lawnmowers off the back of trucks. Ironically, years later it would be a single lawnmower that would turn my life around.

And from time to time I would sell drugs too. Though I wasn't a great dealer because I was way too into trying out my own merchandise. That would send me to state jail for the first time when I was around nineteen. I was at the Hooters restaurant in Addison, Texas, where this undercover informant had set up a transaction to buy fifty ecstasy pills. Call it whatever you want, "criminal's intuition" or something, but I had a bad feeling about it, so I sold him fifty Tylenol instead. You would think I would have just avoided the sale completely since I had a bad feeling about it, but that desperation in me still wanted to make that money, so my warped brain figured I would protect myself by selling him regular old acetaminophen. Nope. They threw me to the ground in the middle of Hooters amongst the smell of hot wings and handcuffed me as I yelled, "Man, it was just Tylenol!" They still didn't

care. They charged me with delivery of a simulated
controlled substance and took me into the Addison Police
Department. When I got there, there was an officer that
sat me down and gave me the old, "well, you messed up
this time, brother" talk. Then he let me know he would
give me an "opportunity" to get out of jail that day if I
agreed to work with them as an informant. There's a
saying the police officers have with informants. They say,
"You bring me three and I will set you free" as in, I rat on
three other people and my charges would be dropped. I
agreed to do it so I could leave jail that day, but I didn't do
it. I never even intended on doing it. And so since I never
brought them anybody, they picked me up again and
threw me in the slammer.

Another time I went to jail was when my friend and I
were leaving a crack house in Southeast Dallas, and we
stole an old Oldsmobile Delta. It was one of those late
seventies big old hoopties. Right after we left the cops
jumped in and started chasing us. It was around 7:00 a.m.
and we're going down Buckner Boulevard, which is a main
street and already pretty busy with morning traffic. And
this car could not do any more than sixty miles an hour
and they have like ten squad cars chasing us and the cops
are pretty much just laughing at us. My friend got freaked
out and started waving his shirt out the window like a
white flag, like "I surrender." But I wasn't surrendering. I
took off running and actually got away for a minute. I
jumped a fence and landed in an ant pile, and the ants got

me, and then the police got me too. The cop actually said I was the fastest white guy he'd ever seen. Maybe I could have done something better with that ability than running from the police. I'll never know. Again, I laugh at myself when I look back at what an idiot I was, but it's not funny looking back on all the years I wasted.

My desire to get high numbed my brain and I stopped stealing lawnmowers or tools or cars and started going straight to the places where the money and dope were. Straight to robbing dope houses.

When I think back on the friends I ran with back then, some of them lived, a lot of them are still in prison, and a lot more of them are dead. I'm about the only one I can think of that actually turned it around. I wish that wasn't the case, I really really do. In prison when youngsters talk about "that life," they're talking about that gangster life. And it's the stupidest shit I've ever heard. Hell no, I'm not about that life anymore. If you're a real gangster, your ass is going to prison or you're going to die. Those are the only two choices. And that's what I tell them when they reach out to me now. The other day a young man called me from the Dallas County Jail. His mom had seen my posts on Facebook, and I was looking at his pictures. He's got a gold grill in his mouth. I'm thinking to myself, *Is that what you think is cool?* Because at one point in time I had one too, and for each their own. But looking back I think to myself, *What the hell was I thinking?* Today, I want to associate with people that care about their lives. What I think is cool are success stories. I don't want a gold grill. I want to drive a Lamborghini with gold wheels. And I'm laughing at myself because I know other people might feel the same about gold grills and gold wheels, and again, to each their own. My point is, what I think is cool has definitely changed. I don't want anything to do with that gangster life anymore. I want some peace in my heart.

Sometimes when I'm in Southeast Dallas to pick up stone and masonry products, I see some of the people I used to run around with. People with junk everywhere; they've got three grocery carts filled a mile high. Or they just look "busted and disgusted" and worn out, and they're walking down the street at seven o'clock in the morning with no shoes on. Or they are passed out in the parking lot of the convenience store. And that could have easily been me. That was me. No, that was dope.

One of my friends from high school was this six-foot-three, half-Italian, very good-looking guy. He was a year younger than me. After high school he went to work at a mattress store and quickly became the number three ranked sales guy. Women went so crazy for him that all he had to say was, "Baby, you look good on my mattress" and BAM! He got the sale! We used to go to this country music club together where they had a "Best Chest" contest. You'd have all these guys on stage flexing and doing back-flips and all my friend had to do was walk across the stage, point and wink at the women, and he would win. He was a pretty boy, totally buff, which he earned by putting in his time at the gym. And it was worth it, because I swear, he had a following. He was literally like a magnet for women. For everyone, really. Just one of those magnetic people that other people want to be around. One of my biggest regrets is that when he was hanging around me he started doing drugs. He was a really good-hearted guy, but once he started using he started doing things you wouldn't normally do. I saw the dope change him. I was pretty strung out at the time. I wasn't at my most down and out, but I was definitely using and losing, and we caught a lot of charges together. We had a total of nine charges: seven misdemeanors and two felonies. I ended up going to prison, but he stayed out by going on the run. He started shooting up heroin and things went from bad to worse, and he didn't end up in prison. He ended up dead. He overdosed in his early twenties. At that time, we weren't even speaking. A bunch of shit had gone down between us and frankly, I was pissed at him. Unfortunately, we never got the chance to make it right. The way he was acting at the end, that wasn't the real him. That was the dope. I grew up with this kid. I knew his family. I knew his mom. He was a mama's boy like me and when he died it destroyed her. This is just one of the guys I can think of that could have done so much with his life. He had what it takes to be successful. And he's not here. He left a daughter behind who is gorgeous and grown now. He would be so proud of her, but she never got the chance to know her dad.

Another friend I lost was a guy I had known way back in elementary school. We did peewee sports together and everything. When we were fifteen he helped me change my birth certificate so I'd be old enough to work at Taco Bell. We ran it through the copy machine, and when the ink was still fresh we erased the last number so it said I was born in 1973 instead of 1974. Though technically a felony, I think this was the most innocent crime I ever committed. By the way, my working at Taco Bell lasted all of about one or two days. But not my friend; he was serious about making money. He was pulling fourteen-hour shifts flipping those burritos at fifteen years old. He went from flipping burritos to flipping houses later in life. He was a total entrepreneur. A hustler. By his early twenties he had two or three tanning salons and a mortgage loan company. But the hustle that funded all these businesses originally was dealing drugs. He ran an extremely profitable business. The thing about my friend was that he never ever did any of the drugs himself. I remember we bought our first sheet of acid together, which is about 100 hits of acid, and four ounces of weed, and we split it right down the middle. We had this massive plan of selling it, making a ton of money and buying more. Of course, I ingested all of my merchandise immediately, but he did exactly what he said he was going to do, and that was the start of his business. So yeah, he didn't do drugs, but drugs killed him anyway. Remember what I said, drugs lead to only two places: prison or death. The worst part is, this guy was actually on his way out of the drug business. He was such a business savvy individual he didn't need them anymore and wanted to be fully legit. He was a good dude with a really good heart. But that didn't matter. He was shot execution-style in his bed along with his fiancé on November 3, 2000.

Those murders have literally just been in the news again because the guy that did it, who happens to be his cousin, has been on death row since 2001. He was supposed to be executed recently but a judge just granted him a delay. The cousin used to live in a big, expensive house, but then he started smoking crack and lost everything. I think the cousin went to ask my friend for money and they got in some kind of dispute, and then his cousin killed them. They said the cousin then stole my friend's Rolex, his Corvette, his fiancé's engagement ring, drugs, and money. But to this day, the cousin still maintains his innocence. He claims it was a rival drug dealer that killed them and that he was framed. I don't believe it. All the evidence showed that he did it. I just hope that man gets right with God. Again another story of a drug dealer and a drug addict that both went down, and the common denominator was drugs. If there's one person I can think of that I would have wanted to save above everyone else, it would have been this elementary school friend. He truly was a decent guy with a good heart. I think how he had all the potential in the world, the sky could have been the limit for him.

Another individual I used to rob with got shot and killed robbing a dope house. My mom would send me the *Dallas Morning News* when I was in maximum security prison in South Texas. I would read all the stuff going on and would see guys I knew getting killed. He took a youngster's dope and the kid killed him. I'll say it again, in the dope game people will shoot you over five dollars.

And there are many times when I shouldn't have made it either. When I was twenty-three years old we went down to Nuevo Laredo, Mexico. A buddy of mine had just robbed a big-time drug dealer and he took me and four other guys down there to celebrate. We did drugs the whole way down, and my body was just worn out. We went down to Boys Town to see the Donkey Show and score some steroids, cocaine, and Xanax. On the way back, somewhere around San Antonio, I realized I was in trouble. I kept telling the guys, man, something's wrong. Something's wrong with me. I ended up curled up on the floor at my mom's house moaning. My brother finally took me to the hospital, and by that time I couldn't move my left hand or arm. It turned out I had had a stroke. I couldn't feel the left side of my body for five days. I was six-foot-three and 161 pounds and completely malnourished. That was a rough recovery too. Still to this day I can't smile right on my left side. And while I was in the hospital my girlfriend was still sneaking in drugs for me. Having a stroke wasn't enough to convince me to get sober either. My girlfriend was beautiful, a varsity cheerleader at her high school, but she got hooked on heroin. She never got the chance to turn it around; she eventually overdosed and died. Another waste of a life.

Another time I probably should have died was during the period I was going out with another girlfriend. One time I was with her and two other guys. One of the guys had just escaped from Rockwall County Jail. Fun fact: Rockwall County is where I do so much of my best work now. It's a really nice area. It feels so crazy to be living a legit life in the same neighborhoods where some of my worst moments went down. Anyway, this guy had just recently escaped, and we pulled into an apartment complex and they had "WANTED" posters of him hanging up. It turns out he was wanted for child molestation. At the time, I had just thought he was wanted for stealing trucks, and that's why I had him in my vehicle, so we could go steal this truck and strip it for parts. There was a Dallas police officer that lived in the apartment complex and he recognized the guy's face from the poster. So the officer called it in, and before I knew it I was running from the Mesquite and Dallas Police in a Mustang 5.0 on Valentine's Day with my girlfriend in the front seat. I had stopped and let the other two guys out, so now it was just my girlfriend and me. How's that for a romantic Valentine's date? They had the helicopter on us and everything, and I got up to speeds of over 140 miles per hour. I ended up flipping the car. It rolled over four times, and we landed upside down on the railroad tracks. I walked away without a scratch. My girlfriend walked away too. Again, sometimes it's hard for me to understand why I'm still alive. Maybe I'm like a cat with nine lives, but if that's the case I think I've definitely used like eight of those nine lives up.

I have so many of these stories. Another time I walked up to a squad car in the Walmart parking lot and knocked on the window. Two police officers sat inside, and I told them, "Y'all gotta stop following me, please!" And they looked at each other and smirked. They didn't even arrest me, just looked at me like I was crazy. I had been up for so many days without sleep and was so strung out, that in my mind everyone was out to get me. I was driving this Monte Carlo with these big old wheels on it and ostrich skin interiors. I've always been a car guy, but my style was definitely different then than it is now. I ended up selling that car to a member of the Texas Syndicate prison gang, and he took me to his connection to get a Mercedes S Class. I had a bunch of money because I was selling a lot of meth at the time. I had that Mercedes for only six hours when I fell asleep behind the wheel with a half a pound of meth in my lap. I woke up to the sound of a Mesquite police officer knocking on the door. So yeah, I got caught with that.

Another time I was robbing a dope house where they were cooking methamphetamines. I had borrowed a gun from one of my friends. It was a Glock forty caliber, actually one of his grandpa's guns. This place where the dope house was reminded me of the David Koresh compound—they had surveillance cameras everywhere. It was two o'clock in the morning, and there was a guy up there on a riding lawnmower. I snuck up and pistol whipped him in the head with the gun, and when I hit him the gun went off. He fell to the ground and I didn't know at the time if I shot him or not. It turns out I didn't. I also didn't notice when I hit him that the clip, the part that holds all the bullets, fell off the gun. I go into the house and I see this guy. He must have been six-foot-five, and he's wearing these overalls, a true hillbilly deluxe meth cook. I grab him and make him take me to where they are storing the drugs in the barn. We get out there and there's a Tupperware bowl full of five pounds of meth. In case you don't know, that's a lot of dope. When I put the gun down on the workshop bench where they were cooking the meth, the hillbilly sees that the clip had fallen off the gun and that it's not loaded, so he grabs a shotgun and points it at me. I grab the dope and take off, running zigzags in the pitch dark while he's shooting at me. I drop the dope and then go back and pick it up. All while I'm still running back and forth trying not to get shot by the bullets whizzing by. I had a guy waiting for me in a car down the street, and somehow I made it out of a precarious situation again. Once again, I probably should not have made it out of there alive.

You know that saying "honor among thieves"? Well there is no honor among drug addicts. Drug addicts will steal your dope and then pretend to help you find it. You know what I'm talking about? "Oh no, I don't have a clue where it went ..." and then, "Let me help you look for it." Especially while on methamphetamines, you can't trust anybody. It plays tricks on your head. You don't sleep and it makes you schizophrenic. Cocaine doesn't let you sleep either. It will make you lose your mind. My mind already races naturally and when I put dope on top of it, it physically wore me out. *Thinking* physically wore me out.

It was just a never-ending cycle. When it comes to the destructive path of drugs, I could tell you stories forever. It made me ridiculously bold. I would dress up as a cop and bust into drug houses and rob them. I jacked and robbed game rooms, which are illegal gambling houses and are also known to be meth hangouts. I have six "evading arrests in motor vehicles" for running from the police. Got some more for trying to evade them on foot. I've gotten beat up by the police several times. Most of the time I put myself in that situation. A couple times I think they "might" have used force that was a little excessive ...

4
BOTTOMED OUT

IN THE TIME SPANNING FROM 1999 TO 2018, I SPENT A TOTAL OF fifteen years and eight months in jail or prison. I think my record totals nine felonies and over thirty misdemeanors. Which means I went in and out of city jails and county jails and prison around forty times. Sometimes, after I got out, I would pick up right back where I started, robbing dope houses and getting high. But other times I would try to straighten out for a bit. Like when I got out of prison in 2009 I did okay for a while. I even got a job driving an eighteen-wheeler. But then I got in a relationship with an ex-stripper and we started drinking right off the bat. That's the thing with me, because I am an addict once I start I can't stop. And as I've said, I go full throttle on everything. So it could start with a Michelob Light on a hot summer day, but then I'll get my buzz on and it's a shot of tequila. Next thing you know I'm doing cocaine and coming up with a master plan like I'm Pablo Escobar. So I'm driving an eighteen-wheeler during the day, drinking and going to strip clubs with this girl at night, and then soon I end up back on dope again. Not only that, I started hanging around a pimp and ended up becoming his bodyguard. This guy was a millionaire, and not that it makes it any better, but the girls he was running were high-price call girls. And I was heavy into steroids at this time, so I'm jacked like a NFL linebacker which is why he liked having me around. Even ripped like that, I wasn't able to guard him from his eventual fate; he ended up in federal prison for human trafficking. And I was back to spiraling out of control. I became a full-fledged addict again by 2010.

When you're living this life, when you're on drugs, no one "normal" really wants you around. I've been everything. I've been a full-blown meth addict. I've been a full-blown crackhead. I've been a full-blown heroin addict. Nothing good came out of any of these things, only chaos. It was a never-ending destructive path I was on and nobody in the legit world even wanted to answer the door when they saw me coming. "Oh no, Buck's coming, turn off the lights and pretend we're not home." Or they would avoid me when they saw me on the street thinking I might rob them. I don't blame them. I was so unpredictable. I didn't want to be around me either, but I had no choice.

A couple times I really did try to quit. And I really did

try hard, but the addiction is so strong it kept pulling me back. Every time I got out I would go stay with my mom and would promise her that I was going to do better, but then I'd go back to drinking or smoking weed. But she never stopped giving me opportunities. The hardest part of sobriety is the first ninety days but the really really hard part is the first ... second ... third ... fourth ... and fifth day. I remember this one time I was so sick from trying to quit heroin. Kicking heroin is the hardest thing physically that I've ever done. And again, when you're going through this, nobody wants to be around you. You are mean and sick and depressed and hurting and probably shitting yourself. I'm sorry to have to say it, but it's true. And my mom, the saint, didn't kick me out when I was in this state, but also, she didn't exactly want to be around me either. Instead, she would just stay over where she was working. At the time she was looking after Ross Perot's sister, on the nice side of Dallas, and she would just stay there. She'd come by the house and drop off cigarettes and Pop-Tarts on the porch like I was a rabid dog or something. I mean, I kind of was. I remember one moment I had run out of food. My mom didn't really have much in the house, and I didn't have a car and nobody wanted to come near me. The only thing I could find were some pecans in the freezer that she had for making pies. And even though I was throwing up and crapping myself, I could somehow keep those down. So, yeah, I want you to visualize this, because if you think you're so tough, you're nothing compared to what coming off heroin does to you. I was all alone, and all I had was a Metro PC phone, one of those really cheap phones, and it didn't even have service. But somehow I could still download songs. I downloaded "Eye of the Tiger" from *Rocky* and "Don't Stop Believin" by Journey and I just focused on those, listening to them over and over again, trying to find the strength in myself to get through it. I'll never forget that because it was one of my lowest moments. But there's been so many low moments.

And then February 24, 2011, it finally caught up with me. I finally picked the wrong drug house to rob. At about 6:30 in the afternoon, I pulled up to this safe house. It wasn't a drug house where you actually go to buy drugs, it's the house where the dealer kept all his inventory. I went up and was about to kick in the door but before I could, a twelve gauge shotgun fired at me from inside. The pellets went through the door and into my arm, but it was just birdshot, so it wasn't life-threatening. But that doesn't mean it didn't hurt—it definitely fazed me! It went through the door and through the Abercrombie & Fitch jacket I had on and grazed my arm. So I took off and got out of there. I went to another house right down the street where I knew a bunch of people. I was there for about twenty minutes when a car pulled up. As soon as I came outside, the two guys in the car unloaded a nine-millimeter and a forty caliber at me from about twenty feet away. The last thing I remember was fire coming out of the gun.

I woke up in the hospital two days later on a respirator and learned that I'd been shot four times, two in the chest that collapsed my lung and went out my back and two in my left arm. I definitely shouldn't have made it through that one. I'm still surprised I did. I actually died twice in the ambulance on the way to the hospital when I stopped breathing. When my mom got to the hospital, the priest told her they didn't think I would make it.

Recovering from getting shot was the worst stuff I ever went through. And I've been through a lot of pain in my life. Going through all my accidents and stitches and stuff has made me pretty tough. But nothing compares to the pain of those bullets going through my chest and out my back leaving a hole in my breastbone. And my left arm was left completely useless. In fact, I'm a left-hander and my left hand is still deformed today. I can't even feel half of it. Like I said at the beginning, even though my injuries were in my upper torso, I couldn't even use my legs again for almost two weeks. And then as soon as I could take a couple steps, they practically threw me out of the hospital on my ass.

By the time I finally did get shot, I had robbed so many people that the police officers at the homicide robbery division in Dallas were not about to put too much effort into finding out who shot me. I can't blame them. The police probably thought like the people in the hospital did, that I deserved it because I put myself in that situation. If you keep playing with fire, eventually you're going to get burned.

And at first, I didn't know who shot me either. But people talk in the dope game. In the drug world, meth addicts stalk Facebook, sit around, smoke dope, and talk about people. You can find out a lot through the grapevine. A friend that I've known since high school was living with this drug runner at the time, and the drug runner told my high school friend that he was the one that shot me. It made sense; the drug runner worked for the drug dealer whose safehouse I had tried to rob that day. So it was retaliation for that, obviously, and I know I put myself in that situation. Four days later, while I was still in the hospital, the drug runner successfully killed a different guy by putting five bullets in the back of his head. Again, that could have been me. Why wasn't that me?

So when I was at my mom's recovering, the drug runner was on the loose and wanted by the police. That's the time people are the most desperate. If you know you are wanted for murder, and you're going to spend the rest of your life in prison, you think killing one more person is going to matter? Or robbing a bank? That's the mentality and that's when people are at their most dangerous. Especially ex-convicts. They have nothing to lose. The drug runner used to drive this white van around. I was glued to the windows of my mom's house, peeking through the blinds, looking for that van. Meth alone will make you feel schizophrenic, but in this case people did really want to kill me, so I guess I wasn't actually paranoid. So when the knock came on the door, logic would tell you it was the drug runner. That's what would have made the most sense.

But here's the crazy part—it wasn't him. See, I had a reputation in the drug world for being a jacker. Robbing people was my M.O. and everyone knew it. At this time this dude who was a captain in the Aryan Brotherhood was trying to find out who robbed his dad. Someone had broken into his dad's house and tied him up and everything. Someone framed me for it, and because of my reputation, the Aryan Brotherhood captain believed them. But this time it wasn't me. I didn't do it. The captain called me and said, "I know you robbed my dad," and I said, "Dude, it wasn't me. I'll come over there and if he says it was me, then come on, do what you got to do." I thought he believed me and that was that.

But he didn't believe me. He made a call to this guy who had just gotten through doing sixteen years in a Texas prison, and he had to spend it all in administrative segregation because he was confirmed in the Aryan Brotherhood. They don't let members of the certain gangs out around the general population in prison to try to cut down on the violence in there. Anyway, he had been caught with nine ounces of the captain's dope. That is the equivalent to about $25,000, so no way was the captain gonna let that debt slide. In the drug world, people get shot up for five dollars, much less over twenty grand. So the captain tells this Aryan member that he will squash the debt if "you go kill Buck." And so that's what he showed up to do.

On that day, as I said in the beginning, when I opened my mom's door this Aryan member put the gun to my forehead, pulled the trigger, and it jammed. Then we tussled, he got the gun back and tried to shoot me again. Then, if you remember, he made a phone call, and I assumed it was the captain on the other end, the guy who had ordered the hit who was telling him to leave. Come to find out the day before, this same Aryan member had kidnapped another guy and his wife. In prison, some guy had gotten the Aryan Brotherhood patch tattooed on him, and this same dude that put the gun to my head kidnapped him and burned the patch off of him. So while he had the gun to my head he was already wanted for aggravated kidnapping.

This is where a U.S. marshal named Kevin, who ironically is my friend and I've known since high school, enters into the story. Back in 2011, I never would have dreamed that I would be on good terms, much less friends, with anyone in law enforcement. He's even currently running for sheriff. Kevin was pursuing this Aryan member for the kidnapping charges; at the time they didn't even know about him trying to kill me. In the pursuit, he used that same gun that jammed when it was aimed at me to shoot at Kevin. Kevin returned fire with an AR-15 and hit him, and the Aryan member sustained life-threatening injuries as a result of that. Anyway, he would go on to get eighteen more years, and his captain would get fifteen years for attempted murder in the aid of racketeering activity, along with other felonies. There was a federal indictment, it's all documented, I even have a Victim Identification Number from Homeland Security because there was a massive effort at this time to bring down the Aryan Brotherhood. Homeland Security, the main guys, came to Kaufman County jail to talk to me. They were part of a special gang task force and were investigating the murders of the district attorney and his wife and another clerk in Kaufman County, and they thought it was the Aryan Brotherhood. So they wanted to know any information I had about the different gangs. Come to find out, it was one of their own county clerks and his wife that had killed the people, not the Aryan Brotherhood at all. It was on "Good Morning America" and everything.

But anyway, this Aryan member goes to jail—and get this—we wind up in the same jail at the same time. But lucky for him he was in administrative medical segregation. When I was in the county jail I was working out a lot and if I ever saw him I planned on giving him what he had coming to him for trying to kill me, but it never happened. Today–looking back–I feel different in my heart. Even though I didn't rob the captain's dad and I didn't deserve retaliation, I am responsible for everything I did that put me in the position to be accused of something like that. I have to take responsibility for it.

I actually forgave the captain through a mutual friend.

I told him to let the captain know that I don't hold animosity. My biggest revenge is success. He's locked up inside and won't get out for a while, but I'm sure he's already seen and heard how my life is going. We were all part of the same messed up dead-end game, and all I want for everyone is the peace with God and the freedom I now have.

But back to that moment. I'm still recovering from my gunshot wounds and someone has just tried, and failed, to kill me again. I felt utterly helpless. So what did I do? I called my mom. Yep. I felt so defeated. She told me to call the police. I'd never called the police before in my whole life. But this time I figured it was my only choice. I wasn't in any position to protect myself if they came back to finish the job. So the police came, they took me to jail for a warrant, and I knew it was the best thing for my safety. I kinda felt like a wussy for even calling the police, because I put myself in that position, being a jacker and a robber and a thug, and NOW I'm calling them for help? But that's what happened. They took me to jail and then they let me out the next day. Looking back, I think about my mom and what that would have been like if she had come home and found her son dead on the floor by the front door only two weeks after almost losing me at the hospital.

So I got out of jail and I went back to my mom's and it's crazy, 'cause it was a never-ending cycle. I was still on the pain pills, and that led back to Xanax. It would always go back to Xanax. Like when you're meth'ed out, after a couple days of being way up and then after a couple days of not sleeping you're all tweaked out, your jaw is moving, you're waving your hands around like a puppet. Xanax would always bring you back down again. But, since I never do anything halfway, I would always take four or five of them and the next thing I knew ... I was going to rob someone again.

So after getting shot and almost getting killed, did I finally decide to change my life? Nope! Instead, I went and robbed another dope house in Forney, Texas. I was all strung out, like big time, and we went to this house at three in the morning. I don't know if you remember The Three Stooges or not, but this pretty much went down like that. We had gone to this dope house earlier in the day, not even planning to rob them. It was a kinda fancy hippie hydroponic weed-growing setup. The funny thing is, today, I do a LOT of landscaping business in Forney. There's a lot of customers that know me there. But I digress; on this day I had gone to buy some weed. This hippie guy there starts copping an attitude with me. He had a real smart mouth, so in my doped-out state I decided, "Well, I'm just gonna come back and rob him tonight."

So at three in the morning, I headed there with a couple of buddies and my girlfriend at the time. We pulled up, and I rolled up on the door and shot it with a twelve-gauge shotgun. Well, I didn't realize they had a reinforced door with a steel core so when I shot at it, the bullets ricocheted back and hit my friend in the face. He's like, "I'm shot, I'm shot!" so I thought they were shooting back at us. Not only did they have a reinforced door, they also had AK-47s. Those hippie nerds were a lot more hard-core than I gave them credit for. It was chaos. We take off and as we are leaving that scene, since we think they are shooting at us, I'm shooting back at them from inside my friend's mom's Suburban that he borrowed for the night. The gunfire blows out the window of the house. Again, this is a really nice, quiet neighborhood. We dumped the car and planned to report it stolen—Larry, Curly, and Moe being stupid. So the shotgun noise brought the neighbors outside to see what was going on. The police were called. They stormed the house and found the AK-47s, pounds and pounds of dope, and the grow rooms. Needless to say, the police took them all to jail. One of the guys I was with ended up ratting on me and to make a long story short, we ALL went to jail. Everybody. I actually felt embarrassed about it because I had gotten away with a lot worse and more dangerous stuff, and then we all went down trying to take this hippie house in a nice residential neighborhood. I heard later, the D.A. had a good laugh at how stupid we all were. Again, being under the influence of a controlling substance gave me bigger gonads to do this kind of stuff.

To me, it was God's way of saying, "You big dummy. I just let you make it through four gunshot wounds, your lung being collapsed, another attempted murder where the gun jammed, and you went and tried to rob another dope house? Well, your ass is going to time out, son. You are going to sit in the corner for six and a half years." Well, the sentence was ten years for a robbery, but I did six and a half of it.

5

LIFE BEHIND BARS

My timeline is a little all over the place, since I went in and out of jail so many times between 1999 and 2018. So here's a rundown of my time "doing time".

When I first went in, it was to Hutchins state jail. I went there for unauthorized use of a motor vehicle, running from the police in a stolen car, and selling those Tylenols to an undercover police officer. When you first get to jail and you go through intake, your money hasn't hit your commissary account yet. It takes two weeks for your mom or family to be able to send you money so you can buy extra stuff besides the three meals they feed you. Soups, snacks, toothpaste, shampoo, all that kind of stuff. There was this guy who tried to run game on me. He told me he would help me out, that he would hook me up with some extra food, some soups and stuff. Then, when it came time that my commissary funds were in, his whole tune changed. He was telling me I owed him this, I owed him that, way more than I should have had to repay him. I told him he was crazy. So we're right in the middle of the day room. I was in C Building 3 Pod 44 Bunk. There are four pods in the building and they are all glass so the guards in the pit can see everything. So everyone was watching as this guy and I were having words and he threatened me. We wore these shower shoes. I flung them off my feet and I hit him with a left. Boom. He went straight on his back. I knocked him smooth out. He gets up and I hit him again with a right-left. This little guy comes up to me after the fight and says, "You need to get out of here, they're gonna jump you." I told that guy to get away from me, 'cause he was a little coward. Mind you, I'm brand new to this. But all it took was me standing up for myself. Turns out he'd been doing this to a lot of people, trying to "hog", as in hog somebody for their stuff. He was a bully, what we call a tank boss. Somebody who acts like they run the whole thing. So I knocked him out in front of 200-plus people. After that I made an announcement. I said, "Look out 3 Pod, I'm not trying to act like a badass, but I'll be damned if anyone takes my stuff that my family bought me." And after that, there was no problem. I can't stand bullies. All the years I was in prison I was in probably eight fights, and all of them were with that type of individual. People are gonna respect you more if you get out there and stand up for yourself. I didn't always win, but I did get respect. The guy's whole tune changed after that. Today, I can't stand owing people money. I pay my debts. But if I'm gonna pay you more than I owe you, that's going to be my choice.

When you're in county jails, you get moved around a lot, and it's actually really stressful. Imagine you just moved to a new neighborhood. You just got yourself situated, figured out which neighbors to avoid, who you could trust. You just got used to your surroundings and your spouse comes in and says, "Hey we're moving to Oklahoma today. Come on, pack your stuff!" As you saw in my experience above, it takes a bit of effort to establish your place inside these units. You're always watching people to see how they carry themselves. To figure out, "Am I gonna have to fight this dude?" There's so many different personalities in there. But once you get settled in somewhere and you're comfortable in your surroundings you can put your guard down a little bit and do your time. That is, until they move you to a new unit again. In six months you're liable to move fifteen times. Not only that, it would have been so much better if I could have done my time flat. My fifteen years and eight months straight through. It was stretched out between 1999 and 2018, getting out, going back, getting out, going back.

And sometimes the unit you get moved to is way worse than the one you came from. The first time I ever hit a maximum security unit I made parole, and I had to take a "Changes" class before I could get released. When I got to this new unit, the whole unit was on lockdown for racial tension. They told me, "You've been assigned to the 'I' wing." "I" wing—they called it "Iraq" because it was so crazy. I walked onto "I" wing with my mattress on my shoulder, seriously, this was like out of the movies, and the whole run was on fire. They had these Johnny sacks, they're the meals they feed you when you're on lockdown that come in brown paper bags. All these papers were wadded up and everyone had thrown them into a pile and it was on fire, smoke billowing up the four tiers of the unit. So the whole unit was on lockdown. All I had to do to go home was complete this three-month "Changes" class. Ninety days, get my certificate, and go home. But since we were on lockdown, I couldn't go to my class. Finally, we got out of lockdown and we went to the day room, and right away, a Crip stabbed a Mandingo Warrior nine times in the neck. The guards did a sweep and found twenty-seven shanks in the day room. So they locked us back down again. We got locked down so often, it took me six months to complete my three-month class. Again, when you're around a bunch of individuals who aren't going home, they don't care. And when you *are* going home, and they know it, it makes you a target.

Prisoners are innovative, that's for sure. Everything in there is homemade. If you burn a plastic razor and you take the soot off of that and mix it with shampoo, you've got tattoo ink. And then they make the homemade tattoo guns out of screws and magnets. All of my tattoos I got in prison this way. I had a celly that made homemade hooch.

He'd put orange juice, potatoes, and yeast from the chow hall into a trash bag. When it started bubbling up, they called it "cooking." It will really get you drunk and leave a *bad bad* hangover too. A lot of people get their heads cracked open after fighting while drunk on that stuff.

The prison system is set up to fail the prisoners. In my experience, most of the time it was the guards bringing drugs and phones into prison. Lots of these prisons are in little podunk towns, and the guards don't make a lot of money, and that's why they do it. You can get five times the street price for selling an iPhone or drugs in prison. So they enable the addicts to stay in the drug life. The convicts basically ran the prison. While I did my longest sentence, I got in good with the convict boss. I guess I was kind of unique 'cause I wasn't part of a gang, but I was cool with everyone. I got along with all the different groups in there. I was a captain's boy, which means I worked for a convict boss who was a captain. This is a position everyone wanted because it gave me so much access. I had access to everywhere on the unit. I was moving cell phones and selling dope. I got hooked, started doing Xanax again, and got caught with dope. I actually took off running from the guard like I was fixing to get away on a maximum security unit. That set me back two years from being eligible for parole.

When you're in prison, sometimes it's a dorm situation where you might be sleeping in a room with fifty people. That's the worst, because you don't have anywhere to get away from all the people. But on the maximum security units, having a good cellmate, we call them a "celly", makes a huge difference. It's like a relationship; you have to respect each other's boundaries. In prison there's always so many people around and the closest you can get to peace is in your cell. One time, I had this celly in Ferguson unit who said he was in for aggravated assault. But he kept telling me he never hit anybody, which just didn't add up because usually that's what aggravated assault is. Then I started finding blood on my razors and my toothbrush had blood on it too. So I told my dad to Google my celly. He found an article in the Fort Worth newspaper that this dude had been arrested because he was going around Fort Worth spreading HIV. He knew he had the diagnosis and he was knowingly spreading it to as many women as he could. The newspaper called him "a snake in the grass." So I got out of there, even though in prison you are supposed to fight it out with your celly and not "tattle". But who is going to fight it out with someone like that? My new celly I got after that was in for raping and killing somebody in the same apartment complex that I used to live in around the same time I lived there. He had a capital life sentence. Moral of the story, you do not want to end up in these places, because you never know who they are gonna put you with. There's some real pieces of crap in there. It's a stupid wicked place and I don't want any more of it.

6

ENOUGH. ENOUGH. ENOUGH.

SOMETHING NO ONE ON THE OUTSIDE EVER TALKS ABOUT IS THERE are actually a lot of really good guys in prison. Yes, there are terrible people as well, but a lot of them are decent guys that could have had great lives, but they made one bad decision, all because of being under the influence of drugs, and now they are in there for life. So being that I was always eligible for parole, I always had it better than a lot of these guys. I also always had the support of my mom and dad. Texas has over 160 prison units, and some of the places I was moved to were a ten hour drive one way from Dallas, but it didn't matter. My parents would always come visit me. It was never even a question. My mom would make that drive no matter where I was. She always sent me money too. Whether I needed it for a lawyer or for the commissary she figured out a way to make it happen. Even in prison, she was still taking care of me. Of course,

I'm sure you can guess by now that I would also use the money to buy drugs. I'd ask for it and she'd get it for me and wouldn't ask any questions. I think the guilt of knowing what it cost her to send me that money and that I was still using it to get high in prison is part of the reason I finally decided to change. I felt guilty because she never gave up on me, but I had given up on myself so long ago.

Christmas of 2015, I'd finally had enough. Enough, enough, enough. I guess I had an epiphany. I don't know any other way to explain it except it was a God thing. I was walking around my cell, high on meth and K2, wanting more, and there was none available. And here it was Christmas Eve, and I was in a maximum security prison for robbing a drug house. Even worse, I was in the disciplinary section of the prison for getting caught with drugs inside prison. And despite all this, I was still getting high. But we had run out, and all I could think about was how I was going to get more. *I think I might have a problem here.*

Living this life is exhausting. The power of a controlling substance will make you do things you would never do before. It will make a housewife into a whore. It doesn't matter who you are. If you allow it to take a hold of you, it's hard to get out of its grasp. On Christmas Eve 2015, I was forty-two years old. I had given drugs almost thirty years of my life. I gave it fifteen Christmases behind bars. Fifteen birthdays. Fifteen Thanksgivings. Out here, the smaller holidays like Halloween and all that don't mean that much. But in there you're like, man, all I want is to be spending Halloween out there. Like that song says, "Don't know what you've got 'til it's gone." And the next day I was like, you know what, I'm going to give myself the best Christmas present ever. Sobriety. And this time I meant it. Boom, everything from this moment went uphill. Slowly but surely I started my climb out of the hole I'd been digging my whole life. I hit my reset button. My mom's prayers were finally answered. It's the single most important decision I ever made.

Luckily this time, the time I finally decided to call it quits for good, the withdrawals weren't nearly as bad as quitting heroin. I was mainly on K2, which is a synthetic marijuana. But the stuff they sprayed on it made it honestly act more like LSD. It had you tripping. I had detoxed from heroin several times before in county jail and like I described before, it wasn't a pretty sight. It's bad. You can't control your bowels. So at least this time was way better than that.

In 2015 I was in the middle of serving that ten-year sentence for robbing that hippie dope house in the residential neighborhood. I had come up for and been denied parole two times already. Every time you come up for parole, you can write a support letter. The first time I was still downplaying what I had done. "Listen, I'm in here for robbery, but no one actually got robbed ... I went to the house and I was about to rob them, but then it ended up going down like a cartoon ..." I still wasn't taking responsibility at all and, needless to say, I got denied. Then the second time I was supposed to come up for parole, I had gotten caught with dope. Denied. The third time, after I made the decision to be sober, I was finally ready to own up to what I had done. I wrote a letter and told them I was guilty and that everything I had ever done was fueled by drug addiction. And I said that I had never been offered help for my addiction but also I had never asked for help either. And that's when they granted me parole and sent me to a prison recovery program. In the state of Texas it's called an FI-5. Different parole programs have different waiting times until you actually get to walk out of the prison; the FI-5 program has a waiting time of six months. When I got there, I really applied myself. It helped that I was sober and things really came into focus. Suddenly I started to see the picture of the life I wanted and was determined to have. At the program there were three buildings, and I worked myself up to the head of one of the buildings. It's kind of like being president of the inmates of that building. It was my job to see over them and handle their problems and disagreements. That was something I had never done before, and it was the first time I realized I could be in a leadership position. I was putting forth a huge effort to be the best I could be. I always had all the ingredients I needed to be successful. But I sold myself short by being under the influence of a controlling substance.

While I was in prison I read a lot of books, I mean, tons of them. It's something I don't have a lot of time for now, but back then I had nothing but time, and some of them really helped me. That's where I first got the idea that if I ever made it through to the other side, I would write a book to help the folks going through the same struggle. And here I am. It actually chokes me up to think about that. Just know if you're there right now, I get it. I was there; I was you. This book is in your hands for a reason. I don't try to ever push my religious beliefs on anyone, but I do believe things definitely happen for a reason and even you have got some guardian angels rooting for you.

I joined a ministry club in prison through the church called Kolbe Prison Ministries. Individuals who had been in our shoes came back in and gave us their time and showered us with love. It was amazing. It's also where I met Damon West, a man who really became like a mentor to me. He'd been through his own addiction and prison and was a living testament that it was possible to turn your life around. He wrote an amazing book, *The Coffee Bean*, and it was so impactful for me. Kolbe Prison Ministries was also the first time I'd heard good Christian music, and it changed me. I really changed inside. I'd be in church and I'd hear these songs and I'd start crying because I knew it was over. I knew I was done with this life. My emotions came back. That's the thing, when you're getting high and living that life, you become kind of like an emotionless shell. Like an observer of your own life, and you stay kind of numb. But once I got sober, it's like the valve got released. Good music will make this six-foot-three ex-con break down in tears still. Once I could feel again, I had more empathy for everyone around me, and especially for my mom.

I remember calling her from the day room. I was in there with all the other inmates. I called her and apologized for everything I had ever done. And I think she knew I was serious, but of course she had every right to be skeptical. Even though I had made promises before—"I'm going to be better this time"—remember, I went to prison four different times before that. I was on my fifth Texas Department of Corrections number. And each time I would do better for a little bit and then I'd fall off because I'd start drinking again or I'd start going to topless bars or start hanging around dope dealers. But anyways, it was during those calls in 2015 after I got sober she told me, "I could tell in your voice that you were serious and sincere." And I think if anybody could tell it would be her. I apologized to others too, people I knew I had wronged. Because for the first time, I could truly feel what I had done to them, and what I had done to myself. And I didn't want to stay there, in those feelings. I needed to make it right and come out on the other side.

So once I got sober and was doing well going through the rehabilitation program in prison, I could start to visualize what my future could look like. I had the idea I could start a landscaping company, and the idea really excited me. I could picture it! I told my celly about it, even my vision for the sick car wrap I wanted to do on my landscaping truck. If you haven't caught on by now, vehicles are my obsession. Once I started letting myself dream big, I started believing I could actually make it happen. And like I said, once I finally got sober, I'd get really emotional. I'd sit in prison, telling myself, *I'm gonna see what this old cowboy can do*. It would choke me up. I had to tell myself that a thousand times.

NEVER TOO LATE
RECOVERING FROM ADDICTION

I can't say enough good things about sobriety. Getting sober changed my life. If you are reading this and struggle with addiction to drugs and alcohol, then my number one piece of advice for you is to get grounded with a program. I can't stress that enough. Whether it's Narcotics Anonymous, Alcoholics Anonymous, or a Bible-based recovery program, do yourself a favor and get plugged in ASAP. It will be the best thing you ever did for yourself.

My second piece of advice for recovering addicts is to separate yourself from people who are also addicts. If you keep running with the same crowd that's dragging you down, it's going to be nearly impossible to escape.

In order to change my bad habits, I had to change my people, places, and things. Once I separated myself from the old and replaced it with the new, I slowly began to take steps in the right direction. We used to have a saying in the recovery programs that I was a part of that you can't keep going to the barbershop and expect not to get your haircut. What does this mean? If you surround yourself with people, places, and things that are negative influences on your addiction, then sooner or later you will give in. You must remove yourself from situations that enable your addiction.

And my final bit of advice—just do it and stick with it. Are we perfect? No. I still make mistakes every day. We all do. It's about how you respond to those mistakes and make sure not to make the same one twice. We can minimize those mistakes, especially the really big ones like substance abuse, by making a commitment to ourselves and to our loved ones that we will change. You know from reading my story that my recovery from addiction was a long ways from perfect. But eventually, I came around and wanted my life to change enough that I put an end to it.

Get grounded in a program. Remove yourself from bad situations. Commit.

7
HURRY UP AND WAIT

So there I was in 2018, ready to face the world. My sober head had a clear vision for what I needed to do, and I couldn't wait to start. I was finally getting released from prison and ready to start my landscaping business. But standing in my way would be a little pesky thing called parole. So that plan was going to have to wait another year.

When I got released from prison, I was basically under house arrest. Since my record was so lengthy they pretty much gave me the most intense parole you can get. I did get to leave the house for certain things, but only under very severe monitoring. I had an ankle monitor on, and another monitor on my waist. I could take the one on my waist off and put it on a charger, but the ankle monitor stayed on all the time. Every Wednesday I'd meet my parole officer, and I had to give her exact descriptions of where I wanted to go. Even something like, "I have to go to the gas station at 11:15 a.m." Then I'd have to tell her the streets I would take to go back home. So there was no way I could start a landscaping company under that kind of monitoring, because I wasn't allowed to go door to door looking for work or to anywhere that hadn't been preapproved.

I tried to get a "regular" job, but as a felon it was really hard to get hired. I'm lucky I had family support when I got out and I know that. I couldn't even get hired to drive a truck lift at a furniture store. Even worse, I couldn't get hired to be a third-shift janitor at a gym. It feels terrible when you can't even get hired to do a job you don't want to do. I understood why people had reservations. Even though I knew I had changed it's hard to convince the people that know and love you, much less someone you just met. And it's a serious problem. When criminals do get out of prison, if they can't get a legit job, what do you think they'll go back to in order to make money? Crime, of course.

So lucky for me, I could stay with my mom. She took care of me again, her never-ending support still astounds me. And I kept her yard immaculate. It was the least I could do, and I had nothing but time! I had a treadmill in the garage I would run on, and I would go to Narcotics Anonymous a lot. I'm not kidding, I would go to meetings three times a day. It was so great to get out of the house and be around people, but also, the program was incredibly helpful for me. If anybody can understand each other, it's a bunch of addicts. You just need to show up and sit down and listen with the mindset of just for today. *Just for today I'm not going to get high.* And then tomorrow you say, *Just for today I'm not going to get high.* They talk about catching ninety meetings in the first ninety days since those are the hardest. The more time that goes by the easier it gets. It's been almost eight years for me at this point, and the good news is that using is the last thing on my mind now. I really do believe in the program even if I didn't totally work it in the correct way. I had a sponsor there, and he was a really good guy. I wasn't your average sponsee. I didn't call like I was supposed to, I didn't read much out of the Big Book. He kinda gave me my own free rein. I shared my testimony there, and it was very therapeutic. I really believe in finding a program or group that works for you.

I was also allowed to go to Lakepointe Church and Celebrate Recovery, which is a Bible-based recovery program. Those were the highlights of my day. I'd be standing there, greeting people in church tatted-up, wearing shorts with my ankle monitor there for everyone to see, and I was so happy just to be there. I'm not trying to push my religion on anyone, but it was really helpful for me. I've gotten so much out of my church. And the music is great; it's like a rock concert. Although I've actually never been to a rock concert, this is how I imagine it would be because there are 2,000 people in that church with the music blasting and everyone is just jamming out.

And my big exciting outing for the week was every Wednesday morning when I was allowed to go to Walmart in Mesquite for one hour to buy groceries. That was a highlight of my life. I would chat with everyone. I did that every week for fourteen months, and I knew everybody there. People would ask me about my ankle bracelet, or I could tell they were looking at it, but everyone was cool. These are just more reasons to not go down this path. You don't want the highlight of your week to be getting groceries at a Walmart.

I hated having the ankle monitor on, but it was much better than being in a maximum-security prison. And I didn't spend time feeling sorry for myself for all the restrictions I had on me during that time. 'Cause at the end of the day, I just knew I put myself in that position and these were the consequences. The thing about it is you do the crime, you do the time. And honestly, I probably should have done more time than what I'd done for everything that I did. So I kept my head down and followed every single rule of my probation to the letter. In prison, everything is so repetitive. When I got out this time, my stomach was tied in knots. The fear of going back in and spending the rest of my life in prison is still to this day what motivates me. And sometimes I had to catch myself, when someone would cut me off in traffic or try to confront me about something. I knew I was only one step away from making a decision that could ruin my life. I always kept that in the back of my head.

Something very significant and very good that happened after I got out of prison this last time was when I opened my Facebook and saw a friend request that made my heart start beating faster. It was this girl Cristi who I knew from high school, though we definitely weren't friends back then. She was the most beautiful girl I had ever seen, but she was way out of my league at the time. I knew I had no chance with her as a scrawny awkward thirteen-year-old pothead. I think I said "hi" to her one time at a party, but we never even had a conversation. I knew who she was, and she knew who I was, but that was it. The last time I had seen her was almost twenty years before at our friend's funeral, and I remember when we saw each other we kinda checked each other out. But then prison put a damper on my dating life for the next twenty years. So I accepted her request on Facebook and we started chatting, and then we started hanging out. When you're on parole, you aren't allowed to go to a restaurant. Not even a drive-through restaurant! I couldn't take her on a date or anything like that. So Cristi would come to my mom's place, we'd hang out, get to know each other, and watch movies. And we've pretty much been together ever since. We did have some ups and downs, and broke up a couple of times for short periods. After all, this was by far the realest and longest relationship I have ever been in. And now I'm so proud to say that she's no longer my girlfriend, she's my fiancé. I "put a ring on it," as they say. So now I have the love and support of two amazing women. My mom and Cristi. I am so thankful for these amazing female forces of good in my life.

I would not be where I am today without these two ladies in my life. On the right is Cristi. And on the left is my mom. Some people have asked me what "periwinkles" have to do with the book. The flowers all around my mom's house are periwinkles. This is my view now that I'm out of prison!

NEVER TOO LATE
POST-PRISON LIFE

Even when you get out of prison, there are a lot of restrictions placed on you because you spent time in prison—such as parole, probation, and restrictions on employment. Even though this is hard for someone just getting out, it's part of the system. Which is why the best piece of advice that I can give to someone fresh out of prison, which I have mentioned multiple times in this book because it is so important, is to do what you're supposed to do.

It will be easy to go back to your old ways. Don't!

Remember: People, places, and things. If you go back to the people, places, and things that put you in prison in the first places, chances are they will land you there again.

There are always going to be obstacles. I always say that things may not go as planned, but we can't give up before the miracle happens. In life, there are controllables and uncontrollables. If you focus on the things you can control, then your time and energy will be well spent. When you let the things you can't control get to your head, that's when you really trip up. It's like when I used to play sports and the ref would make a terrible call. I could yell at them all I wanted but guess what? Refs never change their calls. That's the same with parole and probation. It's their way or the highway. Don't get worked up over it and don't do stupid stuff like I did. Just do what you're told.

We all have tough days. But anyone that's been in prison knows that it's not where you want to be. So when you get out, stay out. Do what you're supposed to do and control what you can control.

8

LIFE BEGINS AT FORTY-FOUR

My ankle bracelet came off April 24, 2019. Free at last! And I wasted no time. Well, other than the thirty years I wasted while addicted to drugs! The very next day, I went to the county clerk's office and registered my d.b.a. for Headz Up Landscaping. Cristi gave me the money to buy a lawnmower, and my mom and dad helped me get a truck. That was the humble beginnings. I put a sign out in my mom's yard that said "Headz Up Lawn Care" and— get this—it got stolen! Isn't that some karma. But it was up just long enough for one lady to get the number, and she called me with my first job. She needed me to trim the ivy from her house. I said yes even though I didn't have a ladder. Luckily the homeowner had one I could borrow, and I was super grateful they gave me the chance. Picture me at the top of a forty-foot ladder trimming ivy and shaking like a leaf because I'm terrified of heights. It

wasn't glamorous, but I was willing to do anything. The
next two jobs were for ladies who worked at my church.
But I learned quickly that mowing lawns was a lot of work
for not a lot of money. I remember I mowed this yard of a
honkey-tonk club near Mesquite. I was trying to avoid
running over glass bottles and needles, and I thought to
myself, "What am I doing?"

Free at last!

So I decided I needed to move more into landscaping. One of the very first times I ever went out to give someone a quote, I went up to their house, a really nice house, and at this time I only knew the name of one kind of flower— begonia. And I didn't know much more than that. I had really only been mowing lawns. So I started kinda just making stuff up. His landscape was already immaculate, by the way, but that didn't stop me. I told him, "You know, sir, we're going to have to do a thorough cleanup of this property and then we should put some ... begonias in here. It will really liven everything up." And I might not have known anything, but he sure did, and he asked me, "Green leaf or copper leaf?" I just stared at him blankly! I'll never forget that encounter, because after I left it took me two days to come up with an estimate, since I had no idea what I was doing. Somehow, I came up with $1,400. And I was never going to get the job because he knew I was bluffing. In the beginning I really was faking it. Back then, I couldn't get a $1,400 job, and today I have a $3,000 minimum.

So the way I got from there to where I am now was by going back to the drawing board and learning more. I studied landscaping. I figured out what the best designs were, and I think it helps that I have "champagne taste". And since I only recognized begonias, Cristi and I would drive around, take pictures of flowers, and make flash cards. I wasn't afraid to admit what I didn't know and to find out about it. Then one of my friends wanted a stone border, and I didn't have a clue how to do that at first. God intervened again, and I got hooked up with Miguel. He is still my partner today. Nobody can touch Miguel on stone borders; he's the fastest and best around. Once we got together it was like a rollercoaster, and we never looked back. Now we could do big-money jobs, and that's exactly what we started to do!

Like I said before, I'm full throttle when it comes to everything. I like the biggest, the flashiest, and the shiniest things that are out there. So nine months after I started the business I Googled, "What's the best land-scaping truck?" And I traded in the truck my mom and dad got me for this brand-new top-of-the-line work truck. It was a four-door, six-seater with a sixteen-foot box on it. And I spent every single dime I had on a car wrap so people could see Headz Up Landscaping coming a mile away. Just like I dreamt about when I was still in prison talking to my celly. It cost $7,000 to do it and, I'm not kidding, it's the best landscaping truck out there. So here I am driving through all the upscale areas of Dallas, by the golf courses and the yachting club, getting all sorts of attention. I pretty much faked it till I made it. 'Cause I didn't have a clue. But I did believe it's all about presenta-tion, and with that truck I looked like I knew what I was doing. Other landscapers were looking at me like, "Where did this guy come from?"

This was the same truck that I would sit in my prison cell and dream about. Seeing it for the first time felt surreal. Hell, it's surreal every time I see it. Invest in yourself and in your dreams. It's never too late.

So once I started doing hardscaping and stonework with Miguel, as I said, things really took off. I went from mowing lawns for twenty dollars to doing $50,000 jobs with water features and things of that nature. My original plan was lawncare, but God's plan was bigger, and today I love what I do. It's hard work, and I've got a great team. But seeing a job come together and the owners' happy reactions when they see it completed? I love that. Yes, the money's great. But I want to be known for my work. My parole officer even reached out to me to do landscaping on her house. It was cool to pull back up to the parole office in my Escalade or my Corvette, which I bought legitimately. I don't have to worry about anybody taking them away from me—not even the tax man, because I stay square with him too. One of my proudest moments was going in and buying the Lamborghini of my dreams, having the cash to put down and getting it in my name. I know some people might not understand, especially if you're not that into cars, but picture the thing from your childhood you dreamt about buying someday if you made it big. Maybe for you it's a yacht, a diamond necklace, a horse. For me it was that Lamborghini. I went from a lawnmower to a Lamborghini. My dream came true.

From lawnmower to Lamborghini. I am living proof that anything is possible!

I think back on all the effort, energy, and work I put into scoring dope. If you can take that hustle, and if you have a lick of sense, there's so much work out here. For me, landscaping was the best choice. There's always grass that's growing, there's always something that needs to be done. People back then were telling me, "Why do you want to open a landscaping company? It's backbreaking work and there are landscaping trucks on every corner." And I said, "But they're not me." I wasn't afraid of the hard work. The thing I was most afraid of was becoming a loser again. I was willing to do anything it took not to wind up back in prison. But now when those same people who told me *not* to do landscaping see me successful, making the money I'm making, they have a different tune. Now they want me to tell *them* how to do it. Well, I can tell you. Get out there and bust your ass seven days a week. That's how you do it. If you call yourself a hustler, put all your hustle and all your game in the legit world and see what happens. You're gonna get out of it what you put into it. And I never forget the fact that I am just one bad decision from losing it all. The devil might try to get in my ear saying, "You can take a toke off that joint, it will help you relax." But I know the truth—I like it too much. It's never going to happen again for me. As much as I liked that, I love this life more.

You gotta look inside and figure out what you could do to get out there and bust your ass. What you can take pride in and turn this shit around with. And then you're gonna get out of it what you put into it. And if it doesn't work, dust yourself off and try something else. With this landscape company we have literally seen blood, sweat, and tears. There have been days that I've cried because I was so frustrated. I was hot, I was busted, I was disgusted. But guess what? I was not going to quit, because my name was on the side of that truck and I had something to prove. I wanted to show people I could accomplish something amazing—you know what I'm saying? And I did. I think more than anything my drive was because I wanted to prove to everybody that I was not a loser. I guarantee you there were a lot of individuals who thought it would only be a matter of time before I was back in prison. "I'll give him six months," or "I'll give him eight months before he starts using again." But I really don't blame them for thinking that. I gave them every reason to believe those things! Well, my biggest revenge was my success. If they don't want you to succeed? Succeed anyway.

I'm at the point now where I charge people just to come out for a consultation, and we're booked out two months. I did over $150K in business just last month. I'm not saying that to brag. I want you to know it's possible. If I can do it, you can do it. If you're sincere with people and have a good heart, people will feel that. I still have all my prison tattoos all the way up my neck, but I'm humble and sincere and honest. My customers put their faith in me, and I'm so thankful. I have a reputation for doing these incredible front yard makeovers, and people pay me for my designs now. I'm proud of that. I've been turning out some really nice jobs lately. My business is about making money, and I make good money. But more important is my reputation and my name and the work that I produce, because I want to be number one in this area when it comes to landscape and hardscape design. Thankfully that's pretty much where I'm headed.

One thing I've learned is that you can't please everybody. Let me repeat that. You can't please everybody. I want to put a smile on everyone's face. And when I finish a job, all my customers are happy. But the potential ones, the ones I give estimates to that go a cheaper route, end up getting what they pay for. Sometimes they call me back out to fix what was done, and then they end up paying even more. Good labor, quality labor is worth the cost.

The best advertising you'll ever get is a happy customer. I don't do any paid advertising; it's all word of mouth and people recommending me on Facebook. I've had to check myself along the way. Keep myself from sending that email when someone gives me attitude. My right-hand man Miguel and I had a love/hate relationship in the beginning. We're both really strong-minded. We've had it out. We've thrown bushes at each other in the yard. Looking back, we laugh at it. Over the past four years we've come to the conclusion that we need each other.

As I mentioned before, some of the best work I do now is in the very same upscale areas where back in the day I did some of my worst crimes. After I turned my life around, I didn't leave and go start somewhere fresh. I stayed right here where the shit went down, and I guess I used that shit for fertilizer. Remember the Lowe's where I stole the chainsaw and tried to return it moments later? I shop there all the time now. They even gave me $20,000 of credit. It feels so good. I recently got out of my Lamborghini in downtown Rockwall, Texas, where Cristi and I were shopping for some furniture, and a guy came up to us and said, "Hey brother, I don't know if you know this or not, but I was one of your arresting officers. I've been following you on Facebook, and I just wanted to tell you how proud I am of you." It made me feel so good. The sun was beaming on my face, the breeze was blowing, my beautiful fiancé and I were standing next to my Lamborghini, and that happened. Talk about a perfect moment. The kind of moment I never would have thought possible in my twenties. Or my thirties. So wherever you're sitting right now take a minute and think about what that dream moment would be for you. Write it down, keep it in your pocket, keep that close to you, because you can make it happen.

A lot of the people from my past are still in that life. They'll call me or hit me up each time they get out of prison. They'll hit me up for money for a hotel room, but I know they're going to use it for drugs. I tell them, you don't need a hotel room. You need a lawnmower. Get out there and start busting your butt. I do my best to give them advice, but I won't be friends with them anymore. Some people you have to love from a distance. I can't associate with anyone still in that life.

I just had a guy call me the other day from inside jail. He needed money to get out after being charged with manufacturing and delivering a controlled substance, which is a pretty serious charge. And he tried to tell me, "Oh man, I was working at a game room because nobody else would give me a job." A game room is a place for illegal gambling, in case you didn't know, and most of them have a lot of drugs and prostitution going through them. And I said, "Man, don't try to sell that shit to me bro. I couldn't get a job as a janitor at a gym or driving a forklift for a furniture store. So you 'had' to go work at the game room. That's just an excuse. What did you think would happen?"

NEVER TOO LATE
FOLLOW YOUR DREAM

In the early days of my business, there was a moment when I was mowing my yard and my neighbor said to me, "Jason, I never thought I would see you mowing your own yard and running a business."

"It's a small yard!" I joked back to them.

I knew what they meant though. The trajectory that my life was on was not a good one. I never forget where I came from. I've had to learn from a lot my past mistakes to get to the place in my life where I am finally doing what I was made to do. I've lived and I've learned.

I was determined to start my own business after getting sober and getting out of prison. I knew that's what I wanted to do. It took time, but I stayed hungry. I focused on getting better and better every day.

I know that if I can do it, then you can, too. Whatever

is holding you back—it's never too late to follow your dream.

9
WHY ME?

I THINK A LOT ABOUT WHY GOD GAVE ME SO MANY CHANCES. Why I've been able to dig my way out when so many others died or ended up with life sentences. It's because I was hard-core. More hard-core than all of them. I see these guys sitting outside, begging for money, and that would never have been me. Even if I had been homeless, I would have gone somewhere and robbed someone. I'm a go-getter in both a positive and a negative way. So I just thank God that I got caught for the robbery when I did. Because if something really bad had happened to someone, I could have easily gone away for life. I've been given a miracle, this opportunity to start again.

From the time I got on my knees when I was in my cell and asked, "Father God, can you please help me with my addiction, please guide me in the right direction to turn my life around?" he heard me. At the time, I believed when

I started helping myself the doors started opening, but looking back, I think God opened those doors.

People reach out and tell me I'm such an inspiration, which makes me feel good, of course, but also makes me think that maybe this is what God saved me for. It's only through his grace that I'm still standing. Maybe he's allowing me to shine in this way so the light can be a guide for you too. God had a bigger plan for me, and I think it's this—the book you're reading now. Even though I don't have that big of a following yet, I hope this book gets to the right places, and into the hands of people who can be helped by it. I have a goal to go on the speaking circuit. I want to tell my story in high schools and colleges. Get to these kids before they make the mistakes I did. My goal is to get to the point with my landscaping business where I have a well-oiled machine and can devote most of my time to this purpose.

And as much as you might feel that people look at you like you're a piece of shit now, let me tell you, people love an underdog story. They love a comeback! Think of every good sports movie ever, and it's all about the underdog beating impossible odds and winning the game! A while back I started sharing my story on Facebook, and it's amazing the support I get. I feel the encouragement there. People are rooting for me! You go to my page, and the first thing you see is "Say Nope to Dope". And I'm real with people. I tell them the truth, the ugly, just like I've told you here. I want people to realize I'm not playing; I'm for real. I have nothing to hide. Some people might be embarrassed that they went to Timberland Psychiatric Hospital for twenty-eight days, or that they were so sick from detoxing they crapped themselves. Sometimes, I probably share too much information. But it's the truth.

I recently spoke at Hutchins state jail, trying to spread the word and give hope. I told them how I went from a lawnmower to a Lamborghini and that anything is possible. It's what I wish people would have told me, because the life I was living was scary. Believe it or not, every single time I got out of prison I had good intentions. I went in and out five times, and every time I wanted to do better. But sometimes I would just plan on "only" smoking weed or "only" drinking. That never worked.

A girl also reached out to me to speak at the Salvation Army. I want to feel like I'm helping others, but sharing my story helps me too. When I speak to inmates or people in halfway houses it really hits home how far I have come. And how dedicated I am to never going back. It helps remind me to appreciate what I have out here. You don't get crab legs in prison. There's no sushi. You're getting Hamburger Helper but they have four different names for it. "Beef stroganoff" one day, "ravioli with beef tips" the next day, and it's all the same stuff.

I just turned forty-nine, and I'm still a big kid. So many years I wasted, from fifteen to forty-one, on drugs. Sometimes I feel like a forty-nine-year-old sixteen-year-old because I'm finally getting to do all the things that I didn't get to do growing up the first time. And I've always loved cars and toys. So now my toys are a lot more expensive. At first, I spent my money as fast as I could make it. I'm trying to be smarter about it now. I want Cristi and me to buy our dream home. But I'm still a big old kid. I take care of my business, but I like to laugh and play and joke. So age is just a number. Well, besides waking up in the morning. I mean my brain and heart are in their twenties, but my back is definitely eighty! I'm still hands-on with my guys and it is hard work; masonry and concrete. And we lift these concrete planter bowls that I buy, and they're crazy expensive, but they're crazy heavy too. They're like 350 pounds a piece, but they're so beautiful.

And I'm not even close to finished yet. I just started a roofing and construction business yesterday. Cristi and I had been talking about it. She was a senior mortgage underwriter for years but was ready for a change. And me, I've always seen all these roofers making bank. One of my friends, Mark, is in recovery too and runs the recovery program for my church. We just spent a weekend away together with his whole family at this lake place. As we were getting ready to leave he was telling me he wanted to leave his job, it's not a good situation for him, so I asked him to come over with me. He has business experience, and I have hustle. So I needed to find a way that made sense for us to be in business together. A while back, someone reached out to me on Facebook and told me I should start a roofing company. Then when Mark came in, it suddenly all came together in my mind. I got the d/b/a yesterday: Headz up Roofing. And then one day later I changed it to Headz Up Roofing and Construction because I ended up bringing in another guy with those skills and connections. I just announced it on Facebook. When I decide to do something, I do it right away. So I feel like I'm being led into expansion in this new area. I guess people appreciate me as "the comeback story", and I really appreciate them. The crazy part is, I'm grateful—super grateful —but still want to do more for my family and friends I'm bringing on board. I'm excited to see how far I can go. Cristi and I prayed on it when we were starting this new business, and then a couple days after we started the area got hit with a crazy hail storm. Softball-sized hail. A storm like that wreaks havoc on roofs, so here we are, off and running. We already have a couple jobs on the books. I'm fixing to see what this new adventure will bring, and I have a good feeling about it.

People go onto my Facebook page and the first thing they see is "SAY NOPE TO DOPE". Then they see pictures of my cars, me changing out the wheels every other week. And they tell me it inspires them. Like, "Man, if this guy can do it why can't I?" A lot of people are scared to fail, or they don't want to put in the work to succeed. The roofing market is saturated, because it's a business with big big profits. But also, a lot of roofers have bad reputations. But I don't care. We prayed over it and the answer came to take the chance. And I'll be honest with people. I've been to prison for drug addiction and I've done good. A long time ago no one wanted to be around me, but now they want to be a part of what I'm doing. It's a good feeling. I feel like if you have good intentions, do the right thing, and don't screw people over, good things are going to happen to you, especially if you put forth the effort. I think back on when I was in prison after I got sober and I used to just talk and talk and talk about everything I was going to do when I got out. I was studying the newspaper, reading about all this construction in North Texas and making all my big plans, and people got tired of hearing about it. Well, one of those guys I used to talk to back then hit me up recently and said, "Man, I've been following you online, and you did everything you said you were going to do!" And that makes me feel so proud I honestly get choked up.

I don't want you to get the wrong idea. It's not like my life is perfect now. Nah, I work hard! And I still have shitty days and I get mad and I lose my temper. Today I've been up since 4:30 a.m. Someone stole my truck. When you have flashy wheels and stuff like that, people take notice. And hey, how mad can I get? Maybe it's karma again. But anyway, it was in the shop getting fixed, and the guy there left it unlocked with the keys inside. I posted on Facebook that it got stolen, people shared it almost four hundred times, and some random guy found it in a field. But it was kind of cool, 'cause there was a little puppy out there that somebody had abandoned, and it was exhausted and miles and miles away from anything. So it probably wouldn't have lived if it hadn't been lying there right by my truck in the grass. So yes, I believe that everything happens for a reason. Unfortunately, a lot of things are hard to understand; death and tragic accidents and things like that. But I do believe in angels and the law of attraction and the higher power.

And when stuff like that happens, like when my truck got stolen and I got really mad, I know that turning to drugs or alcohol isn't an option for me, because I'll lose everything. I already know. I've already played the tape.

10

MY HOPE FOR ME AND MY HOPE FOR YOU

MY STORY IS FAR FROM OVER. I STILL HAVE SO MUCH I WANT TO achieve and experience. One thing I've never had the opportunity to do is travel the world, and I'm so ready to. I want to get my business to the point where I can do that. I want it to be able to run itself to the extent that Cristi and I can take off on an Alaskan cruise or on a train through Switzerland. My life might seem glamorous if you look at my fancy cars and stuff, but day to day I'm grinding. Usually, I'm working from 6:30 in the morning until 6:30 at night, and after that I come home, do a couple of estimates, then maybe put on a movie and immediately fall asleep. For me it used to be about the Lamborghini and things like that, but maybe I finally am growing up, because now I know that isn't ultimately what's going to make me happy. I want to experience things. I want to enjoy life. All the "things" in the world won't make you happy, because happiness comes from inside. I know that now. I'm over the cars and all that. I never thought I would say that. Well, I'll probably keep the Lambo. It's my trophy. But I'm done spending money recklessly. I went for so long not being able to have things that I went a bit hog wild, but going forward I have different priorities.

I don't know what the future holds, but my other big dream is to someday be a part of my children's lives. I purposely haven't gone into any details about them in order to protect their privacy. I wasn't any type of father to them growing up, and have absolutely no expectations they would ever consider me a father figure now. Both of their moms are good women, and I was abusive to them. I hate to admit it, but it's the truth. They deserved to be treated so much better than I treated them, and I'm truly, truly sorry about all of it. I was a totally different person than I am now. I never would've done anything like that if I wasn't under the influence. And that's the truth, because I'm telling you that dope will completely change a person. I totally understand if they never want to be a part of my life, and if that's the case I accept it, because I take responsibility for being a selfish, drug-addicted idiot who only cared about chasing dope. But if somehow my kids read this please know how very sorry I am and that I own my failure completely. I apologize for not being there. I would take it back if I could, but I can't. I'm sure you've heard a lot of stories about me, and I'm sure ninety-nine percent of them are true. Just know that wasn't me. It was me under the control of an addictive substance, and I'm never going back there. I have the utmost respect for your moms and whoever else helped raise y'all. If you ever want to open that door to any type of relationship, I would love that. I don't want to intrude in your lives, and I respect whatever you're feeling, but I still hope this message finds you. I didn't get to be a good father, but I'd love the chance to be a great grandpa. I'd love to buy the kids all the cool toys. I'd be really into that.

And to anybody that I've ever hurt, robbed, stolen from, fought, or put my hands on, I really want to ask for your forgiveness. And likewise I forgive anybody who's ever done anything to me. A lot of people ask, "Why would you forgive somebody that shot you in the chest?" Well, for one, I put myself in that position, so I don't hold any animosity about it. In addition, unforgiveness is not healthy. Part of working the steps in the Narcotics Anonymous book is making amends and letting go. And sometimes letting go is hard, but it's the best thing to do. To anybody still in prison that had anything to do with me, look at me. I'm telling you, my life is so good now. And if I can do it, you can do it. It's never too late.

All I can do is keep going down the right path and try to make every day better than the one before. Sometimes it gets tempting to dwell on all the bad things I did in the past, but doing that doesn't help anybody at this point. I'm fixing to make this world a better place, and I want to make everyone's lives around me better too.

Start doing the right things, and you'll feel better even
before you see the results. You've got to just take it one day
at a time. There's help out there. There's Narcotics Anonymous, there's Alcoholics Anonymous, there are Bible-
based recovery programs. All the help is out there today if
you want it. Catch ninety meetings in your first ninety
days. Put yourself around like-minded individuals. There
are so many success stories to hear when you go into
Narcotics Anonymous, and you know what they say, birds
of a feather flock together. Get in with those people that
are trying to do the right thing. If you're really sick and
tired of all the negativity that drugs have caused you in
your life, then give recovery a try. If it's not dope that's a
problem for you, take the first step to overcome whatever
your addiction is. If you're overweight and start going to
the gym, you're gonna start feeling better about yourself
long before you get six-pack abs. And that's what I want
people to understand. It's never too late to start your new
life. When I made that choice to stop using drugs in
prison, I automatically felt better about myself. I don't feel
like I'm a totally unique story; nobody should put me on a
pedestal by any means. If you hit that reset button and get
on the path, it will work for you too. It sounds morbid, but
think about your funeral. If I had kept going down that
path it would have been a lot of, "Well, he was a good
dude when he was sober, but the struggle finally got him."
Nope. I want people to say, "Man, this dude turned it
around. He was a good man. He helped everybody in his

path. He did amazing work. He was inspirational." But don't get the wrong idea—I'm not ready to go yet!

So I'm back again, your ex-thug-hugs-not-drugs substitute mom saying I hope you can find that unconditional love for yourself that a mother has for her child. Love yourself enough to give yourself a chance. And as for my mom? That's the best part of all of this—how proud I make my mom today. Now she's always bragging about me to her friends. I'm able to buy her a Louis Vuitton purse and do things at her house, but none of that will ever equal the unconditional love she showed me from day one. I pulled into QuikTrip the other day and there was this guy hanging out there who was so spun out. I gave him twenty dollars and said, "Don't use it for dope, brother. Get something to eat." That could have been me. If my mom would've turned her back on me, I would've been homeless many times. Like I said, a lot of inmates that get out, their families give up on them. But she never did, and I thank God for that. So this book is dedicated to her. I put her through hell, and she would've taken a bullet for me. Literally when there were people trying to kill me she refused to leave.

Here's what I want you to take away from this: if this guy can do it, then you can too. I don't have a lot of business smarts. I don't. But I make up for it with drive and hustle. You don't have to be smart. But you do have to stay consistent and bust your ass. I do think about where I could have been if I had never gone down the path of addiction, but who knows. I probably wouldn't have had the fire under me I have now. Would I have been a slacker? A stoner? Someone who just half-assed everything? Who knows, but I'm not going to fail now, and I don't have a minute to spare. I'm still fixing to see what this old cowboy can do. I feel great, and I want more. I want to take it to the next level. Every single good thing I have comes down to the decision I made to get sober on Christmas Day 2015. Every single thing. There was only one decision that could lead to the road out.

Are you thinking about hitting that reset button? If the thought scares you I get it, I really do. Maybe you're afraid you're not strong enough to succeed. Maybe you've already tried five times and failed five times. I know so many of you are trapped in that cycle. I know you want to quit; believe me, I know. I still can't believe how many things I had to go through until I was finally ready to be done for good. Nine times out of ten, you have to hit rock bottom before recovery will stick. For me it was like that scene in *Forrest Gump* when he finally stops running. He's just done. I was just finally done. I don't know if it was a God thing, but it hit me: If I don't change, I'm going to spend the rest of my life in prison. I was sick and tired of being sick and tired.

I missed out on so many opportunities with how much time I spent in prison. So much life! Getting sober and getting out of prison were two of the best things I ever did. Now, I'm living life to the fullest.

Only you can decide when you've really had enough. Let's face it, if anyone else could have decided what my rock bottom was, it would have been way earlier. Like when I went to prison for the first time. Or when I had a stroke on the way back from Mexico. Or when I got shot five times, and then two weeks later someone else tried to kill me. Any of those would have been completely appropriate "rock bottoms". But that's the hard part. Someone else can't make you change. So if you're reading this book because you have a loved one stuck in addiction, and you blame yourself that you haven't succeeded in getting them out of it, stop that blame game. It's not your decision, unfortunately.

If you are the one that needs the reset, and you feel like you've messed things up so colossally, to such a degree that it could never be repaired, I get that too. And now here's some advice. I'm telling you, the reset button still works. The reset button doesn't judge. Doesn't only work if you've been "sorta" bad or "didn't really mean it." It's there whether you use it or not. Now you might have a deeper hole to dig yourself out of than someone else. It might take you a long time to climb back out and feel the sun on your face. But you might as well start climbing. You can't change your past, but your future hasn't been created yet. You *will* be creating your future one way or another. Doing "nothing" about a problem is still making a choice. So what's that choice going to be—ten, twenty, thirty more years of the same? Life is always going to be hard, so what do you want your hard to be? Staring at the door of your prison cell? Staring into your mom's or loved one's eyes and knowing you disappointed them again? Staring at your empty bank account and wondering how you're gonna get the money for your next hit? Or staring yourself down in the mirror, looking yourself in the eye and telling yourself that you are gonna take it one day at a time, and today, your "hard" is gonna be working hard for the life you want.

Here's some final advice and encouragement: If you get out of prison and are on probation or parole, just do what you're supposed to do. If you don't, you'll make your life a lot harder than it needs to be. Just get through it. Getting a job with a criminal record isn't easy. I know that. A lot of doors were shut in my face, but they weren't God's plan. My advice is to start your own business. It was the best thing I ever could have done. It won't be easy. Anything really worth having isn't easy. But you can do it if you give it all you've got. And believe me, it's so much better on the other side. If you want it bad enough, you can make it happen. It's never too late to start over. I'm rooting for you. I really am. Hit that button.

NEVER TOO LATE
FORGIVENESS FROM YOURSELF AND OTHERS

Sometimes, we hurt people when we screw up. I certainly did. Family, friends, co-workers, neighbors... the list goes on and on. But a lot of times we forget about the harm we do to one pretty important person: ourselves.

In my story, I was lucky enough to have a mother that welcomed me back into her arms. Some people aren't that lucky. Some people burn all of their bridges. Which is why, no matter your situation, it starts with you. *You* need to be able to forgive yourself for the harm you've done. Once you can adopt this mindset, you can begin to make changes and earn peoples' trust back.

There is not a one-size-fits-all solution to earning someone's forgiveness. Nor should there be. Depending on what you did and how you hurt someone, there may be lots of layers to it. But one quality that can improve everyones' chances for forgiveness is this: sincerity. Being genuine. Meaning it.

It's easy to tell when someone is being fake. No one wants a fake apology! Ten times out of ten, that puts you further back than where you started.

That's why I believe it all starts with forgiving yourself. Once you own up to your mistakes and recognize your wrongs, that's when your heart and mind can really start to change. That's when you can really be sincere with yourself and others in your journey to forgiveness and fixing your relationships.

It's much harder to go through life alone than it is with people who care about you. I could very well still be at the lowest of lows without my support system. Look yourself in the mirror, own up to your mistakes, and forgive yourself. Then seek the forgiveness of others. And if you're lucky enough to have people that love and support you despite your screw-ups, then lean into that! Understand that you are blessed to have those people in your life.

ACKNOWLEDGMENTS

I would like to say thank you to everyone on my Streamline Books publishing team who helped me along the way. A special thanks to Jeannie, Alex, Trevor, Annika, and Hannah for going above and beyond to accommodate my schedule. Thank you to my dad and Bonnie for the weekly encouragement and support; to Cristi, my fiancé, for her unconditional love and voice of reason; and to Miguel, Jeromy, Chikki, Lewis, and Miguel Jr. for helping me make the Headz Up Landscaping team what it is today. I also want to thank Mark (aka Roady) and Shelley H. for always pushing me to write this book. And, last but not least, I want to thank God for listening to all my prayers.

ABOUT THE AUTHOR

Jason Head is a nine-time convicted felon who has spent over fifteen years in Texas Prisons. From the age of fourteen, he has struggled with the worst of drug addictions, which landed him in juveniles, youth villages, psychiatric hospitals, and emergency rooms.

On December 25, 2015, in a maximum security prison unit in South Texas, Jason decided to give himself the best Christmas present ever—Sobriety. After being released on parole in 2018 at the age of forty-four, he started a landscaping company that has found great success. He continues to inspire others that it is never too late to start over.